BROAD GAUGE
RAILWAYS

Tim Bryan

SHIRE PUBLICATIONS

Bloomsbury Publishing Plc
PO Box 883, Oxford, OX1 9PL, UK
1385 Broadway, 5th Floor, New York, NY 10018,
USA

E-mail: shire@bloomsbury.com

www.shirebooks.co.uk

SHIRE is a trademark of Osprey Publishing Ltd

First published in Great Britain in 2018

A catalogue record for this book is available from the
British Library.

ISBN: PB 978 1 78442 277 6
        eBook 978 1 78442 284 4
        ePDF 978 1 78442 283 7
        XML 978 1 78442 282 0

18 19 20 21 22   10 9 8 7 6 5 4 3 2 1

Typeset by PDQ Digital Media Solutions, Bungay, UK

Printed and bound in India by Replika Press Private Ltd.

Shire Publications supports the Woodland Trust, the
UK's leading woodland conservation charity. Between
2014 and 2018 our donations are being spent on their
Centenary Woods project in the UK.

COVER IMAGE
The reconstruction of 'Firefly' at Didcot Railway
Centre. (Alamy)

TITLE PAGE IMAGE
The interior of Fox's Wood Tunnel on the original
Great Western Railway main line between Bristol and
Bath.

CONTENTS PAGE IMAGE
A beautiful photograph of 'Iron Duke' class 4-2-2
'Amazon'. Built at Swindon in March 1852, this and
other engines of the class were principally used on
broad gauge express services between Paddington and
Bristol.

ACKNOWLEDGEMENTS
Images are acknowledged as follows:

Author's Collection, pages 4, 8, 11, 12, 13, 14 (both),
19 (top), 20 (both), 24, 27, 29 (both), 32 (bottom),
33, 34, 40 (bottom), 41 (top), 46 (both), 46 (bottom),
48, 49, 54, 55, 56 (both), 60 (bottom left), 61, 63;
Geoffrey Tribe, page 58; Getty Images, pages 9, 16, 19
(bottom), 36, 47, 60 (bottom right); iStock, page 30.

All other images are courtesy of STEAM: Museum
of the GWR, Swindon. Thanks are due to Felicity
Jones and Elaine Arthurs from the museum for their
assistance in sourcing images. The author would also
like to thank Brian Arman of the Broad Gauge Society
for his help in checking and correcting the text.

CONTENTS

IN LOVING AND REGRETFUL MEMORY OF
THE BROAD GAUGE

Died May 20th, 1892

On May the twentieth a train
Was speeding o'er the sweet Thames plain
    Upon the Broad Gauge Line.
And from the whistle moans arise
That rend our hearts ; and loud she cries,
    " O, woeful fate is mine ;
Next morn to Swindon shops I go
Where hammers clank and forges glow,
Where I was born scarce four years past,
And yet this trip shall be my last ;
    ' Great Western ' is my name.
I thought to run for many a year
Upon the line whose name I bear
    And win for swiftness fame ;
But now my trav'ling days are o'er
This track shall know me now no more."
She spake, and as her plight I spied
In wrath " Ye Fools and blind " I cried
    " O brutal, bungling, Board
That dare Brunel's great work undo
A greater man than all of you
    And hope thereby your hoard
To heap on high with L.S.D.
May ruin ruthless rout your glee.
Brunel's sad shade I see it stand
With Gooch from Clewer, hand in hand
    And scan the Iron Way,
Not bright and polished as of yore
By thund'ring trains with rush and roar,
    But rusting in decay."

      *   *   *

Next morn in sorrow rose the Sun,
He saw with shame the deed was done,
    Broad Gauge had passed away.

INTRODUCTION

A T 5PM ON 20 May 1892, the final broad gauge train to depart from Brunel's great station at Paddington made its way westward, meeting the last service in the other direction, the 5am mail train from Penzance, at Teignmouth. It was reported that as the trains stood next to each other, passengers joined hands through the carriage windows and sang 'Auld Lang Syne' to mark the demise of the broad gauge. This outpouring of affection was not an isolated incident and crowds had already assembled at a number of other stations during the course of the day, demonstrating the popular feeling about the passing of this Great Western institution.

In the months following the final conversion of the broad gauge all manner of glowing tributes were paid to it, but Brunel's bold experiment had not always engendered such high praise. Engineers, shareholders and subsequently railway historians and enthusiasts were and always will be divided over the merits of the broad gauge. The history and fortunes of the Great Western Railway were inextricably linked to its decision to adopt the 7-foot gauge, long after its final removal in 1892, and the effects of the fateful decision not to build the railway to Stephenson's standard gauge would ultimately cost the GWR much in terms of increased costs and decreased shareholder dividends. Reporting the conversion in June 1892, the journal *Engineering* concluded that 'all must feel a regretful interest in seeing the last of a bold experiment carried out in the teeth of vehement opposition, and brought to success, at least for a time'.

OPPOSITE
Following the end of the broad gauge, a number of affectionate tributes to Brunel's experiment were published in both prose and poetry form. This particular poem was subsequently reproduced in a GWR publication in 1935.

ANATOMY OF THE
BROAD GAUGE

When Isambard Kingdom Brunel was appointed as
the engineer of the new Great Western Railway in
March 1833 he still had much to prove. While his reputation
had grown following his success in winning a competition to
design a new bridge at Clifton in Bristol two years earlier, the
chance to work on a railway to link the city with the capital
was vital to cement a career still in its infancy.

In early 1831, members of the Bristol business community
met to discuss 'the expediency of promoting ... a railroad
from Bristol to London'. Having seen the success of the
Liverpool and Manchester Railway, opened a year earlier, the
idea made good business sense and it was agreed that a first
step should be a survey of a route for the new line. Brunel,
although known to many in the city, was not assured of the
job and found himself in competition with a number of other
engineers who had already worked on railway schemes locally.

The selection process was that each engineer would
survey a route, with the cheapest estimate winning the job;
characteristically, Brunel argued that this was unacceptable and
that the promoters of the railway were 'holding out a premium
to the man who makes you the most flattering promises'.
Brunel would provide the best – not the cheapest – route,
he contended, a risky strategy bearing in mind his relative
inexperience as a railway engineer. Gambling on the reputation
he had already gained while in Bristol, his strategy paid off,
although his appointment was approved by only one vote.

OPPOSITE
Isambard
Kingdom Brunel,
the architect of
the broad gauge,
photographed
at the launch of
his steamship
SS *Great Eastern*
in 1858.

Brunel was paid just £500 to survey a route for the new line, now called the Great Western Railway, a process that took several months to complete, with much of the work done by Brunel himself, with the assistance of W.H. Townsend, a Bristol engineer. Despite the creation of a prospectus in 1834, it took two attempts to steer the Great Western Railway Act through Parliament, with Brunel spending many hours in committee, justifying various aspects of the railway's design and construction. As the engineer formulated designs for the railway, it soon became apparent that what he called 'the finest work in England' would not be a carbon copy of any railway then in existence, and would incorporate more than its fair share of new features.

Brunel's sketchbooks are full of his thoughts on the railway's operation, including details of bridges, stations, tunnels and trackwork. In public at least, however, Brunel revealed little about the track gauge to be adopted. Some indication that change was afoot could, though, be gathered by the fact that he was able to persuade Lord Shaftesbury, Chairman of Committees at the House of Lords, to omit the normal clause

Broad gauge zenith: a GWR postcard showing a 'Rover' class 4-2-2 hauling the 'Flying Dutchman' express near Uffington in 1890.

in the Great Western Railway bill formally defining the gauge of the railway.

Until this point, the question of gauge had been of little consequence to railway engineers or shareholders. The 'standard gauge' (4 feet 8½ inches) adopted by railways built until that time was a result of the fact that most of the railways and tramroads serving mines and ironworks in the North East of England, now seen as the cradle of railway development, already had a track gauge of around 4 feet 8 inches. As many of these early lines were horse-drawn, the gauge was traditionally determined by the width of a carthorse and the size of the wagon it could haul.

When George Stephenson was appointed as engineer of the Stockton & Darlington Railway in 1821, he chose a gauge based on his experience of working in collieries in the Northumberland coalfield; Killingworth Colliery, where he designed and built his first steam locomotive, had a track gauge of 4 feet 8 inches, and so not surprisingly the SDR followed the same pattern. The 'standard' gauge became truly standard when Stephenson also chose it for the Liverpool & Manchester Railway which opened in 1830.

The opening of the Stockton & Darlington Railway on 27 September 1825. Crowds watch the first train, hauled by 'Locomotion', driven by the railway's engineer, George Stephenson.

The Grand Junction and London & Birmingham railways, also engineered by Stephenson, followed suit, as did railways that connected to them.

The somewhat haphazard way the standard gauge had evolved must have been one of the factors considered by Brunel when he revealed his proposals for the gauge to be adopted on the GWR in a report to the directors a month after its bill had passed through Parliament. The report recommended a 'deviation from the dimensions adopted in the railways hitherto constructed'; Brunel's new line would be a high-speed railway, with gentle curves and gradients reducing friction between rail and wheels using a wider gauge of between 6 feet 10 inches and 7 feet. By adopting a wider gauge, Brunel argued that carriages and wagons could be built that had bodies mounted between the rails, lowering their centre of gravity, further reducing friction. The report did warn that the wider gauge would cost the company more money as it would entail bigger cuttings, embankments and tunnels as well as the potential 'inconvenience' of making

Brunel's ambition to build a new railway with gentle gradients and curves is well illustrated with this lithograph by J.C. Bourne showing the approach to Chippenham station.

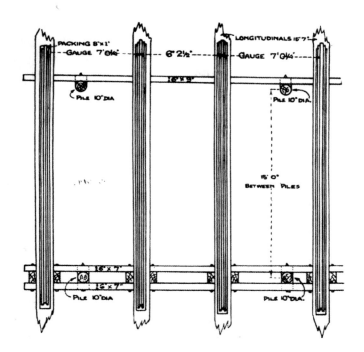

A GWR plan showing the original layout of Brunel's baulk road. The piles, fixed at 15-foot intervals, were soon removed to improve the quality of ride for passengers.

a junction with the London & Birmingham Railway, with whom the GWR hoped to share a London terminus.

The adoption of what became known as the 'broad gauge' was approved by the GWR board in October 1835, although this news was not made public until August 1836, when shareholders were informed of the directors' decision to recommend an 'increased width of rails'. Not content with this dramatic innovation, Brunel also had his own ideas about the formation of the track itself. Early lines, such as the Liverpool & Manchester and London & Birmingham, had used stone blocks fitted with iron chairs supporting the rails; travelling on the former in 1831, Brunel had been singularly unimpressed by the rough ride and instead opted for his own solution. Rails were supported along the whole of their length using 30-foot longitudinal sleepers, with cross sleepers (known as transoms) fixed at 15-foot intervals. Ballast was

The new broad gauge track utilised 'bridge rail', in the form of an inverted 'U'. The profile of the rail can be clearly seen here, showing its reuse as a fence post near Charlbury station in Oxfordshire.

forced under the whole structure to support the track, which was then bolted on to beech piles driven into the ground. All timbers were 'Kyanised', an early form of timber preservation, which predated the use of creosote. Another departure from existing practice was the rail itself, an inverted 'U' profile known as 'bridge rail', which was fixed to hardwood planks and bolted directly on to the sleepers.

The whole arrangement was both more expensive (£500 per mile more than stone blocks) and more difficult to install, and this, coupled with poor weather, meant that building the railway took longer than Brunel and the directors would have liked. The first section of line between Paddington and Maidenhead did not open until 4 June 1838, and while there was much public enthusiasm, with more than 100,000 passengers travelling on the railway between June and August, the smooth ride promised by Brunel was not evident. The track settled, and the method of pinning the track down with timber piles transformed the line into a switchback, creating what one observer called a 'see-saw' motion. The rough ride was compounded by the poor build quality of the carriages, which had bad springing and wheel tyres of differing thicknesses.

These teething problems, exacerbated by an inadequate and unreliable locomotive fleet, did not go unnoticed by Brunel's opponents, who were quick to argue that his extravagant claims about his new railway had not been justified. Brunel faced particular criticism from a group of shareholders based largely in the North of England nicknamed the 'Liverpool

Party'. While the poor performance of the railway was the initial focus of their discontent, the question of the broad gauge and Brunel's competence soon became apparent, and in August 1838 attempts were made to dismiss him. While many on the board were sympathetic, they bowed to pressure and asked other prominent railway engineers to inspect the new line and make recommendations.

Two reports were compiled by Nicholas Wood and John Hawkshaw, but neither produced enough conclusive evidence to convince the directors to abandon the broad gauge entirely, although both were critical of many aspects of the operation of the new railway. Hawkshaw in particular had little good to say about the broad gauge, and argued that any company not adopting standard gauge was in danger of isolating itself, a claim that would be repeated years later. Replying to this criticism, Brunel admitted that the gauge question was 'undoubtedly an inconvenience' but added that since the GWR was being built in places where 'railways were unknown', once his broad gauge network was completed, no other lines would be needed, avoiding the problem of areas where two competing gauges might meet.

The broad gauge baulk road as reconstructed by the Great Western Society at Didcot. In this case the formation is of 'mixed gauge' track with a third rail laid to allow standard gauge trains to operate.

The 1925 replica of 'North Star', the Stephenson 2-2-2 that hauled the first train on the GWR. The original engine was unaccountably scrapped by the company in 1906; the reconstructed engine survives at the STEAM Museum in Swindon.

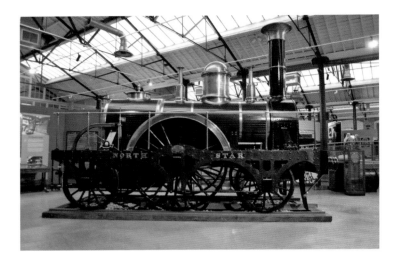

Wood also argued that the broad gauge was a more expensive proposition and that the railway built so far could be converted at a cost of £123,976, and the GWR could save a further £156,000 by completing the rest as a standard

The size and scale of both trackwork and rolling stock are well illustrated in this undated postcard view of a 'Rover' class 4-2-2 hauling a train in the West Country.

gauge line. Armed with an array of statistics and costs, Brunel was able to disprove these arguments, although Wood's more thorough study of both broad and standard gauge locomotives highlighted the disappointing performance and coke consumption of Great Western engines, even the seemingly reliable and powerful Stephenson locomotive 'North Star'. Wood attributed this to the greater air resistance faced by broad gauge engines, but following experiments and modifications to the engine instigated by Brunel and his locomotive superintendent Daniel Gooch, dramatic improvements were made to both performance and fuel consumption.

Armed with news of these improvements and other evidence, at a special shareholders meeting on 9 January 1839 Brunel was able to weather the storm generated by the Liverpool Party. While the proceedings were described as 'very stormy', with opinions as 'wide as the poles asunder', the directors recommended 'retaining the gauge … as most conducive to the interests of the company'. To improve the ride, they also ordered that the use of piling be abandoned and that a heavier type of rail should be used. Shareholders agreed, although by a margin of 7,790 to 6,145 votes, hardly a ringing endorsement of the engineer or his broad gauge experiment; for now the gauge question had been settled, although not conclusively, and Brunel could concentrate on the important task of completing the railway itself.

Another view of the 'Rover' class, providing a rare glimpse of the ample dimensions of the locomotive footplate.

BRUNEL'S GREAT WESTERN

ORK ON THE original Great Western Railway between Bristol and London had begun soon after its Act of Parliament received Royal Assent. The construction of the line was divided into separate contracts for different stretches of line or particular projects, such as bridges, tunnels or stations, each built by different contractors. For the next six years Brunel supervised all aspects of the project, producing drawings and specifications, consulting with contractors, landowners and engineers and travelling up and down the line checking the work. The original budget had been £2.5 million, a figure that in hindsight was hopelessly optimistic; Brunel's new railway was grand in conception and construction and his new broad gauge did not come cheap. As one contemporary commented, 'it would have been a matter of surprise if the original estimate had been anything like adequate to the purpose'.

As already noted, the opening of the first section of the line from Paddington to Maidenhead had been delayed. In addition to problems caused by new track and unreliable locomotives, the company's original plan to share a terminus at Euston with the London & Birmingham Railway had foundered. Negotiations proved fractious from the start; an unwillingness to offer the GWR anything more than a five-year lease on station facilities was bad enough, but matters were made worse when Brunel's decision to adopt the 7-foot gauge was announced. The arrangement was abandoned and a new station was planned

OPPOSITE
Brunel's genius as an architect and engineer was critically important to the success of the GWR, but the blood, sweat and tears shed by the thousands of navvies who laboured to build it cannot be overestimated.

The temporary station at Paddington is well hidden behind Bishop's Road Bridge in this early lithograph of the terminus. The bridge also housed ticket offices and other facilities.

at Paddington instead. Brunel had produced designs for a substantial London station, but financial difficulties meant a rather more modest 'depot' was built to serve as 'a temporary station for passengers until permanent buildings can be erected'. These premises, described as a 'dark and dirty wooden shed', would last for more than fifteen years. Situated in a cutting behind Bishop's Road Bridge, the station was a jumble of railway lines, arrival and departure platforms, two carriage sheds and a locomotive depot. When the first trains ran in June 1838 the new terminus was not yet finished; work continued on and off until 1845, and its final appearance was in stark contrast to Hardwick and Stephenson's station at Euston.

In 1850 the directors finally made funds available to allow Brunel to construct a station on a scale befitting its position as the Great Western's headquarters. The new terminus was situated east of the original buildings in a cutting, so much attention was paid to the design of the train shed roof. Brunel's final design was made possible by advances made by Joseph Paxton, the designer of the Crystal Palace and inventor of a 'Patent Glazing' system that revolutionised the construction of large glass roofs. Already busy with other projects by this time, Brunel enlisted Matthew Digby Wyatt, another engineer involved in the Great Exhibition, to produce decoration for the roof and glazed screens of the train shed.

Difficulties with the main contractor meant that work on the project was slow, and building the new station and removing the old one at the same time led to Paddington being opened in two stages – departure platforms completed in January 1854, and arrival platforms opened five months later. Although operational, the station was far from complete, and the complex was not properly finished for another three years.

The geology and geography of the route planned by Brunel meant that contractors working at each end of the line faced very different challenges. At the London end, the line traversed the River Thames a number of times as it ran westwards. At Maidenhead, Brunel designed a striking bridge featuring two graceful 128-foot semi-elliptical spans springing from a central pier, reputedly the largest and flattest ever built, which allowed the railway to cross the Thames without restricting river traffic. The design was controversial and triggered the kind of criticism the engineer would endure throughout his career. Brunel was undeterred when experts cast doubt on whether the bridge would stand. His critics were given more ammunition when poor workmanship by the contractor allowed brickwork to distort before it had set properly. The fault was rectified and the bridge, despite all the

Detail of the train shed roof at Paddington station. Brunel's second London terminus remains one of the most important survivors of the broad gauge era, and retains much of its character, despite the inevitable changes brought about by new technology.

Rain, Steam and Speed – the Great Western Railway. This famous painting by J.M.W. Turner captures a GWR train in full flight travelling over Brunel's Maidenhead Bridge.

This Edwardian postcard captures the graceful lines of the Maidenhead Bridge. By the time the card was posted in 1907, the river was used for pleasure traffic and the barges that plied the Thames with goods were long gone.

uproar, did not fall down; it survives today, albeit much widened.

Further west, the line ran through a 2-mile-long cutting at Sonning. Excavation of the cutting turned out to be a huge battle against the elements, with more than a thousand navvies and 200 horses struggling to move thousands of tons of spoil in miserable winter weather. Brunel was forced to manage the project personally following the bankruptcy of the contractor and a strike by the navvies, but by March 1840 trains from Paddington were able to run through the cutting and on to Reading. The station there featured what one GWR historian described as a 'curious' layout that typified Brunel's determination to create a railway unlike any other built thus far. When the railway reached Reading, the bulk of the town was on the south side of the track, so the station was a strange one-sided affair, with up and down tracks having their own separate platforms, each with its own booking office at the east and west ends of the station. The unorthodox track layout made the station very complicated to operate, although it was not rebuilt until 1895, two years after the end of the broad gauge.

Beyond Reading, Brunel's railway ran on through the Vale of the White Horse, and by December 1840 the line had been completed as far as Hay Lane, 3 miles west of Swindon. There

A plan of the single-sided station at Reading, which was in effect two separate terminals.

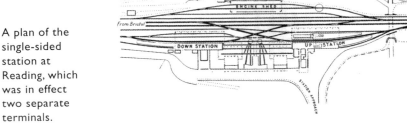

was no station in Swindon itself; this was not finally ready for passengers until 1842.

For the engineers, navvies and contractors working at the Bristol end of the line, the most formidable challenges were faced travelling further west. In contrast to the gentle gradients found east of Swindon, the line towards Chippenham and Bath was characterised by steep gradients and the high embankments and deep cuttings that went with them. The wet weather experienced by contractors caused the clay making up the embankments to slip, necessitating expensive piling to stabilise them. Beyond Chippenham, Brunel faced his greatest challenge. After passing through the 3-mile Corsham cutting, Great Western broad gauge trains plunged through the 2-mile-long Box Tunnel. Driven through 2 miles of limestone and fuller's earth, when completed in 1841 it was the longest railway tunnel in the world, and the 400-foot-high Box Hill under which the thousand or so navvies laboured for four years was a formidable obstacle.

At the committee stage of the GWR bill there had been much discussion about the tunnel and the safety of passengers travelling through it. Described as 'monstrous

A rare and early photograph of 'Aries', a Gooch 'Leo' class locomotive pictured at Chippenham shed. Built by Rothwell's of Bolton in 1841, 'Aries' was not withdrawn until 1871.

The interior of Box Tunnel, as recorded by J.C. Bourne, not long after its completion in 1841. Although this lithograph shows the tunnel as being unlined, for most of its 2-mile length Box was lined with brick.

and extraordinary' by one critic, another argued that its construction would lead to 'the wholesale destruction of human life'. For many to whom the idea of rail travel was still a great novelty, the concept of travelling through the tunnel must have seemed frightening. Stagecoach operators were able to tap into this nervousness, illustrated by an 1841 advertisement for the 'Star' coach in a Bath journal that noted that 'Persons fearful of Box Tunnel may go to Chippenham by this coach and proceed in the 11 o'clock train'. After five years of construction, the tunnel finally opened on 30 June 1841, the last section of Brunel's broad gauge line to be completed, enabling trains to run through from Paddington to Bristol.

If the expense and difficulties of building Box Tunnel and other earthworks between Chippenham and Bath were not enough, a further obstacle was encountered at Sydney Gardens on the outskirts of Bath. A massive retaining wall was required to support the Kennet and Avon Canal, which also ran through the city on a similar route. As the railway passed through Bath itself, it ran largely on embankments, crossing the River Avon twice. The station as constructed had an overall roof and was built 'in the style of James the First with debased gothic windows', as one contemporary described it, its elegant frontage facing into the Regency city.

The short stretch of line between Bath and Bristol also contained more than its fair share of engineering work, including seven tunnels, numerous deep cuttings and embankments. When the GWR reached Bristol in 1840 it was arriving in a thriving maritime and industrial city. While Bristol businessmen had played a pivotal role in the creation of the company, it was surprising that its main station was situated at Temple Meads, a mile or so from its commercial heart.

An undated but fascinating photograph of Box station, some time before the abolition of the broad gauge in 1892. Although the banking engine is standard gauge, mixed gauge trackwork remains in evidence.

The terminus built by Brunel there was in the Elizabethan style and consisted of a castellated frontage, with the train shed built on a viaduct at first-floor level. Passengers bought their tickets on the ground floor and then ascended steps to the platform and must have been greatly impressed by the spacious interior, which boasted a 72-foot-wide mock hammer beam roof, built in the style of Westminster Hall in London.

The full opening of the Great Western Railway from London to Bristol on 30 June 1841 was marked with little ceremony, the novelty of railways probably having worn off in Bristol. By the end of the year, Brunel's 7-foot gauge had spread further with the leasing of the Swindon to Cirencester section of the Cheltenham & GW Union Railway and the completion of the first section of the Bristol & Exeter route to Bridgewater, increasing the broad gauge network to more than 172 miles.

Brunel's terminus at Bristol. The main station building housed ticket offices and a board room for directors' meetings; on the roof was also a large tank to enable locomotives to take water.

Mr Barlow And Mr Mills And Thomas H. R.
Poynder Esq, by which the Company agree to
purchase certain portions of Mr Poynders Land that
will be required for the Railway for £1600 and
to construct the Line through his Estate as therein
mentioned.

_____

7th April 1847 =   Between Charles Russell Esq
                   F. P. Barlow and E W Mills Esq
And His Grace The Duke of Northumberland for
the construction of The Railway through His Grace's Est
in the manner therein mentioned

_____

15 April 1847 =   Between The Great Western
                  Railway Company and Thomas
Wilmot Esq - by which the Company agree in
the event of their obtaining their Bill to purchase
certain premises at Egham Hithe for £2500

BROAD GAUGE EMPIRE

IN JANUARY 1845, the directors and shareholders of the Great Western, Bristol & Exeter and other railways with whom he had been recently employed presented Brunel with a special gift. Described as 'handsome centrepieces and candelabra, side dishes and salt-cellars' valued at 2,000 guineas, this token of esteem was reward for his efforts. While few doubted the scale and quality of Brunel's GWR, the fact that the railway had been completed late, and at a cost far exceeding the £2.5 million estimate, was not forgotten by his critics. Brunel was not without detractors, a correspondent noting in 1865 that many of his schemes were 'freely, and we might say, warmly criticised by those shareholders who, being opposed to the broad gauge, objected to the extra expense which it entailed'.

The completion of the Bristol to London line in 1841 was the first in a series of broad gauge railways that in Brunel's own words would 'monopolise all the West'. As early as December he noted in his diary that as well as the GWR he was also working on the Bristol & Exeter, Bristol & Gloucester, Cheltenham, and Merthyr & Cardiff railways, and the Newbury branch (which he dismissed as 'a little go, almost below my notice'). In 1847 the 'Railway Mania' was in full swing and Brunel's portfolio had grown enormously. New schemes were set to extend its reach across the country; west of Bristol, the Bristol & Exeter, South Devon & Cornwall and West Cornwall railways would ultimately link the Royal Duchy with the capital, while broad gauge tentacles spread into Wales

OPPOSITE
After the completion of the GWR in 1841, Brunel's railway work took him all over Wales, the West Country and the Home Counties. This 1847 document, listing various land transactions in the London area, bears his distinctive signature.

This historic image illustrates not only the eastern end of Brunel's train shed at Bristol, but also the rather less imposing wooden station built for the Bristol & Exeter Railway, situated at right-angles to the GWR main line.

from Gloucester and the Forest of Dean via the South Wales Railway. Other railways ran north from the original main line to Cheltenham and Oxford and the Midlands.

The number of railways being built meant that Brunel could not work as he had done on the original Great Western. More than 1,000 miles of broad gauge line were completed before his death in 1859 with the help of a long-suffering team of draughtsmen, surveyors and assistants, although he still maintained a characteristically high level of supervision of all these projects. Given the large number of schemes promoted, there is simply not space to describe them all; what follows does illustrate the development of Brunel's broad gauge empire. Many lines were not built by the Great Western but by associated companies with their support, the common link being that their engineer was Brunel.

By the time the GWR had opened fully in 1841, the next link in Brunel's plan to spread his system westward, the Bristol & Exeter, was already well advanced. Trains ran from

Bristol to Bridgwater, but Exeter was not reached until 1 May 1844, when the opening was celebrated 'amidst tremendous rejoicings'. Although planned as an extension to the Great Western and operated under lease by them until 1849, the B & ER was an independent company and not finally absorbed by the GWR until 1871.

The Great Western and Bristol & Exeter companies were allies when it came to support for the next railway to continue Brunel's network west. Both provided capital for the South Devon Railway, authorised in 1844 to link Exeter and Plymouth, its route skirting the Devon coast and climbing over the foothills of Dartmoor. Although the sharp curvature and hilly nature of the route undoubtedly provided Brunel with engineering challenges, it was a broad gauge railway remembered more for Brunel's use of a radical new type of propulsion – the 'atmospheric system' – rather than its gauge. In 1844, the only working atmospheric railway was the Kingstown & Dalkey in Ireland, and after a visit there Brunel was able to convince the directors to abandon his original plans for a doubled-tracked line worked by steam locomotives, instead proposing a single-track route utilising the atmospheric system.

Work began in 1845, but despite the completion of the line between Exeter and Teignmouth by May 1846, progress on the installation of the atmospheric system was slow, and the line was initially operated by steam locomotives hired from the GWR. Trains using the new system finally ran in February 1847, but more than a year later, the 'Atmospheric Caper' had proved to be a liability to the SDR. Continuing problems led to the suspension of the atmospheric system in September 1848; by January the following year, shareholders abandoned it,

A reconstruction of the way the South Devon's atmospheric railway track would have been installed when the ill-fated system was tried between 1846 and 1848. A leather flap was riveted to the top of the pipework – greased to ease the passage of trains, it was attacked both by salt water and rats attracted by the grease!

A section of the South Devon Railway near Dawlish after the removal of the atmospheric system but before the replacement of the baulk road with more conventional cross-sleepered track.

the debacle costing the company more than £400,000, with the additional expense of having to re-equip the line for steam operation.

Passengers were finally able to travel from London to Plymouth via the South Devon in April 1849, but Brunel's dream of running broad gauge trains from the capital to Cornwall would not be realised for another decade, and he would not live to see the railway reach Penzance. The GWR, Bristol & Exeter and South Devon railways, subsequently known as the 'Associated Companies', all provided support

PENRYN VIADUCT

A sepia postcard view of one of the timber viaducts employed by Brunel on many of his Cornish projects. This one at Penryn, between Truro and Falmouth, was finally replaced with an embankment in 1923.

for the Cornwall Railway, linking Plymouth and Falmouth more than 60 miles west. The new broad gauge railway gained parliamentary approval in August 1846 but had a difficult start. Always short of money, the challenging route chosen by Brunel had no fewer than thirty-four viaducts on the 53-mile stretch of line between Plymouth and Truro alone. As a result, most were constructed of timber, a cheap and quick alternative to masonry.

The most difficult obstacle for the railway was the crossing of the Tamar at Saltash, and initially at least, the company concentrated on building on the Cornish side of the river. Work stopped when the 'Railway Mania' bubble burst, and only recommenced in 1852 when the original plan to build a double-track line was replaced with a cheaper single-line option. The final link in the chain was the opening of the Royal Albert Bridge, completed in May 1859. Brunel's bridge had taken seven years to build and cost £225,000, underwritten by the Cornwall Railway's investors. The line from Plymouth to Truro was officially opened on 5 May 1859, but trains did not reach Falmouth for another four years.

The most westerly section of Brunel's broad gauge network was the West Cornwall Railway.

A Cornwall Railway luggage label. The name of the final destination was rather too long for the printer to accommodate on the labels, so has been shortened.

244   **C. R.**

Passenger Luggage.

Bodmin Road to

Launcestn

The act authorising the company had been passed on the same day as the Cornwall Railway but it had a more complicated history. As well as building a new route from Truro to Penzance, the company also acquired the Hayle Railway, an 11-mile standard gauge line dating from 1837. The new line was built as standard gauge too, with a proviso that it would provide a broad gauge rail with six months' notice if required. Penzance was reached in 1852, and when the Cornwall Railway was completed in 1857 the GWR gave notice to the WCR that it wished a broad gauge rail to be installed to allow through trains to run. Unable to comply, the 'Associated Companies' therefore took over the line in 1865 and set about adding broad gauge rails; by 1 March 1867 Brunel's broad gauge had finally reached Penzance.

The building of a line linking Paddington and Wales had been delayed, as it had in Cornwall, by the completion of a Brunel river bridge. The South Wales Railway had

Major strengthening works were carried out on Brunel's Royal Albert Bridge between 2011 and 2014 and it continues to be a vital part of the Great Western main line.

been authorised in August 1845, but building the line was complicated and drawn out. Financed largely by the GWR, with Brunel as its engineer, the broad gauge railway was originally planned to run from Standish near Gloucester, along the South Wales coast to Swansea, and then on to Fishguard. The financial troubles shared by many Brunel railway schemes also beset the SWR and meant work was initially concentrated on the 75-mile section between Chepstow and Swansea opened in June 1850.

The proposed line to Fishguard was abandoned and the railway eventually ran to nearby Neyland, reaching there in 1858. Meanwhile, at the other end of the line, a new scheme to link the railway to Gloucester was devised using a junction at Grange Court. This and the rest of the South Wales main line remained separated for almost a year, while the final link, a 300-foot single-span bridge across the River Wye at Chepstow, was built. Brunel's structure – a combination of cast-iron tubes and suspension chains – was probably a test bed for his later design for the Royal Albert Bridge. Construction was advanced enough to allow single line working in July 1852, with both tracks complete the following year. The construction of the

A serious accident on the main line of the SWR at Bullo Pill on 5 November 1868, the result of a mail train from New Milford crashing into a cattle train from Carmarthen. Cattle carcasses can be seen on the side of the track.

Stonehouse on the Cheltenham & Great Western Union Railway featured a chalet-style building typical of those used by Brunel for smaller locations and was recorded by a postcard photographer in the early part of the twentieth century.

SWR was ultimately to cost the Great Western dearly; almost all other railways promoted to capitalise on the expansion of the coal industry in South Wales were standard gauge, and had no direct connection to the GWR, resulting in much of the lucrative coal trade going elsewhere.

Gloucester was also on the route of another broad gauge offshoot of Brunel's original Bristol to London main line. The Cheltenham & Great Western Union Railway ran from

The original timber train shed at Frome. Completed in 1850, it was designed by J.R. Hannaford for the Wilts, Somerset & Weymouth Railway, fully opened in 1857. The station remains one of the earliest in regular railway use.

Swindon to Stroud and on over the edge of the Cotswolds to Gloucester and then Cheltenham. The first section from Swindon to Kemble and Cirencester was opened on 31 May 1841 and immediately leased to the GWR to operate. The company struggled to raise money to complete the most difficult part of the route and was ultimately purchased by the Great Western in 1843, the line being finally completed two years later.

There is not space to do more than mention other broad gauge lines such as the Berks & Hants, East Somerset, Wilts, Somerset & Weymouth and Wycombe railways, along with branches such as those linking Bridport, Calne, Faringdon and Moretonhampstead, to name but a few. Brunel's 7-foot gauge even penetrated deep into the centre of London, shortly after the death of the great engineer. The Metropolitan Railway running between Paddington and Farringdon Street opened in 1863 as a mixed gauge operation, as was the Hammersmith & City line completed a year later.

The Brunel station building at Culham, on the Didcot–Oxford line, seen in 2017. When the station opened on 12 June 1844 it was called Abingdon Road; it was renamed in 1856, when the nearby Abingdon branch line was opened.

DEATH OF THE BROAD GAUGE

THE ST IVES BRANCH was the last to be built to Brunel's broad gauge. Completed in 1877, the 4½-mile railway that ran between St Erth and the West Cornwall resort of St Ives was nevertheless an anomaly, as the Great Western board had recognised more than a decade earlier the need to finally replace the broad gauge and had been actively planning its abolition. Brunel's death in 1859 had also prompted GWR management to finally contemplate the end of the broad gauge; as the staunchest defender of his bold experiment the engineer would certainly have put up a vigorous fight at any attempt to remove it during his lifetime.

Although Brunel's close friend Daniel Gooch had been a strong advocate for the broad gauge, by 1865 he was Company

The promotion of the Oxford, Worcester & Wolverhampton Railway was one of the flash points for the beginning of the 'Gauge War'. Charlbury, situated on the section of route between Wolvercote Junction and Worcester, was finally opened on 4 June 1853.

Chairman and realised that to survive the railway needed to convert to standard gauge. Supporters of the broad gauge managed to postpone that momentous decision, particularly after the outcome of a Royal Commission held in 1845 to decide on a uniform gauge for the whole country. The disagreements about the merits of the broad gauge first aired when it had been introduced in the 1830s had not disappeared, and as the network was extended, criticism of what became known as 'breaks of gauge', locations where broad and standard gauge lines met, grew louder. By the time of the Royal Commission there were ten stations where passengers were forced to disembark and transfer themselves and their luggage from one system to the other. The transfer of goods was similarly inconvenient, with the process often taking between four and five hours.

The extent of Brunel's broad gauge network, along with the places where a break of gauge took place (marked with a black dot), are recorded on this map, to which an unknown hand has added the date '1845'.

The whole issue became known as the 'Battle of the Gauges' and was further exacerbated by competition between the GWR and rivals like the London & North Western; the promotion of a number of new broad gauge lines, including the Bristol & Birmingham, Oxford & Rugby and Oxford, Worcester & Wolverhampton railways provoked fierce opposition, and the government finally moved to end the controversy by appointing the Royal Commission to investigate.

Commissioners began gathering evidence on 6 August 1845, and over the next thirty days supporters of both broad and standard gauge appeared to argue the advantages of their respective systems. Brunel appeared on 25 October 1845; he answered a total of 200 questions on a variety of subjects

A cartoon, showing the 'Break of Gauge' at Gloucester, one of the places where broad and standard gauge lines met.

but characteristically, when asked if he would make the same decisions again, maintained that whilst he might be accused of recklessness, he should 'rather be above than under seven feet now, if I had to reconstruct the lines'. Arguing convincingly about the technical advantages of the broad gauge, he was less convincing on the question of a uniform gauge for the whole country and the 'break of gauge' problem. This was especially strange for a man with such vision, who had designed steamships to link continents, but he seemed unable to admit railway passengers might want to travel from one side of England to the other, instead characterising railways as a series of competing regional networks.

When the Commission finally reported in 1846, it was the question of a uniform gauge that was seen as most important; it ruled that 'uniformity be produced by an alteration of the broad to narrow gauge', a decision supported by the telling statistic that in 1845 only 274 miles of broad gauge track were in use compared with 1,901 miles of standard gauge. The announcement was angrily denounced by Brunel and supporters of the broad gauge who mounted a vociferous defence, eventually forcing the government to water down legislation by inserting a clause in the bill that ensured all railways built in the future would be standard gauge unless their railway acts had a 'special enactment defining the gauge'.

This concession was only a stay of execution, and opportunities for expansion were much reduced. As Britain's railway network expanded, the GWR found it harder to maintain its regional isolation, and the unique nature of the company changed as it began to acquire standard gauge companies. The West Midland Railway, taken over by Great Western in 1863, was an amalgamation of a number of companies, including the Worcester & Hereford and Oxford, Worcester & Wolverhampton railways, which added a substantial standard gauge mileage to the network.

The addition of standard gauge trains was a complication, and to overcome the difficulty of working trains from one

Close to the end of an era: standard and broad gauge trains await departure in the gloom at Paddington.

system to the other, the GWR introduced the 'mixed gauge', providing a third rail between existing broad gauge trackwork, which allowed standard gauge trains to run on the same lines. By the 1860s the broad gauge had expanded to more than 544 miles, with an additional 78 miles of mixed gauge line. While an ingenious solution to a difficult problem, the mixed gauge was not a long-term solution, and the tangle of pointwork at busy stations must have been a challenge for operational and track staff.

Mixed gauge track was ultimately only expediency on the part of the GWR while it prepared for the complete removal of Brunel's broad gauge. Converting the network in one operation was not an option; while the sheer scale and technical complexity of the task and inconvenience to passengers was a factor, the company simply did not have the money to complete the work immediately. Instead, after 1869 lines were converted as funds became available. The conversion of the 22-mile Hereford, Ross & Gloucester Railway in August of that year provided the company with valuable lessons, containing as it did tunnels, curves and gradients along with all types of broad gauge trackwork including baulk road and cross-sleepered track. Above all, the experiment showed that preparation was vital, along with large numbers of men to 'attack the whole line at once'.

Section by section, the broad gauge was eradicated from the network; the pace of change increased significantly in 1872, when the route between Swindon and South Wales and associated lines in that area were converted. Two years later the Wilts, Somerset & Weymouth suffered the same fate. In 1886, Gooch told shareholders at the company that the end of the broad gauge could not be postponed for long; passing away three years later, he did not live to see its end, and by 1890 all lines were either standard or mixed gauge, 'pure' broad gauge only remaining on the Chard branch, between Exeter and Falmouth, and on branches west of Exeter. By July

Great Western Railway
LOCOMOTIVE DEPARTMENT.

CONVERSION OF GAUGE
BETWEEN READING AND HOLT JUNCTION,
Including the Marlborough Branch.

NOTICE TO ENGINEMEN AND FIREMEN.

Every Engineman working over the above-mentioned Lines, during the Conversion of the Gauge, will be supplied with a copy of the printed TIME TABLE AND GENERAL INSTRUCTIONS issued for the use of the Company's Servants, for which his signature will be taken. No Engineman must on any account take charge of an Engine or Train on any part of these Lines after June 26th, or subsequently during the Conversion, who has not previously received and signed for, the Time Table and General Instructions.

The Enginemen are requested to make themselves thoroughly acquainted with the Time Bill and General Instructions, and they will be expected to read them through with great care as soon as they receive them, and if they meet with anything which they do not properly understand, or which they think requires explanation, they must at once apply to their Superintendent, or Foreman, or one of the Locomotive Inspectors on duty, in order that there may be no misunderstanding whatever on the part of the men engaged in this work.

The particular attention of the Enginemen is directed to clause 18 of the General Instructions on Page 6 as to stopping " *dead* " at the end of each Section ; also to Clause 23 on the same page. ALL FACING POINTS MUST BE APPROACHED WITH VERY GREAT CAUTION, and at the Crossing Places the greatest care must be taken to have the Engine or Train so under control, as to prevent the possibility of overshooting the Points.

Enginemen and Firemen must keep a constant look out for any signal that may be given by the Permanent Way Men or others, whether by means of a Red Flag or other Hand-signal : They are to proceed with great caution, especially on approaching curves, when they must take care to sound their small whistles, so as to give timely warning of their approach to the men working on the Line.

Enginemen and Firemen are particularly requested to be with their Engines in good time, and to bestow the greatest care upon the oiling and examination of the working parts, Axle Boxes, &c. They must be particularly careful to have a good supply of coal before starting from each end, and to fill up their tanks at every watering place, so as to be fully prepared for any unexpected stoppage or delay. So much depends upon the Engines being in the best possible working order, that it is hoped very great attention will be paid to this matter, MORE ESPECIALLY WITH THE NEW NARROW GAUGE ENGINES.

Firemen are also required to make themselves well acquainted with the Time Table and General Instructions, and the Enginemen must afford them every opportunity of doing so. As far as possible the Enginemen and Firemen should read the Instructions TOGETHER, so as to obtain a perfect knowledge of them before commencing to work the single line.

J. ARMSTRONG.

Engineer's Office, Swindon.
22nd June, 1874.

A handbill issued by the GWR to footplate staff regarding the conversion of the Berks & Hants section of the railway in June 1874, warning staff to ensure they had enough coal and water to cope with any 'unexpected stoppage or delay'.

1891 only the latter remained as final remnants of Brunel's broad gauge system.

The final conversion took place in May 1892, when the remaining 177 miles of track were altered to 4 feet 8½ inches. Months of preparation ensured that the massive operation to remove broad gauge was successful, with more than 4,000 navvies used to complete the task in a single weekend; they were accommodated in goods sheds, stations and even tents

A rather posed photograph showing the final conversion of the broad gauge near St Germans, Cornwall. The picture shows the preparatory work done with transoms already cut so that the rail could be slewed over by permanent way staff.

along the line, and careful planning meant that following the last day of broad gauge operation on Friday, 20 May 1892, work was completed in only thirty-one hours. By Sunday, 22 May, the broad gauge was no more and the following day

An illustration from the *Graphic* magazine of 28 May 1892 showing the 'platelayers and surfacemen at work in the early morning on the line at Saltash'.

The *Graphic*'s account of the gauge conversion reported that men were accommodated in a camp between Plympton and Cornwood.

standard gauge trains were able to run, with a full passenger timetable in operation twenty-four hours later.

Part of the meticulous planning required was to ensure that all broad gauge locomotives, carriages and wagons were retrieved from depots and sidings and sent to Swindon for conversion or scrapping.

Some idea of the sheer scale of the task facing Swindon Works following the final extinction of the broad gauge in 1892 can be seen in this photograph of sidings containing carriage stock.

BROAD GAUGE SWINDON

Before the coming of the Great Western Railway, Swindon was described as a small market town 'set upon the summit of a moderate hill' at the western end of the Vale of the White Horse; in later years the GWR would describe old Swindon as 'an ancient market town of some note'. The route of the new Bristol to London line passed north of the town in an area of farmland; Gooch's diary records that the area was still 'only green fields', and the rather unremarkable landscape was described by the writer Richard Jefferies as 'furze, rushes and rowen'.

By December 1840, Brunel's railway had reached Wootton Bassett Road, a temporary terminus 2 miles west of Swindon at Hay Lane. There was as yet no station in Swindon itself, a state of affairs that would last only five months, as Brunel and Gooch finalised their plans to establish a railway complex at 'New Swindon' – a place that would include workshops, a station and a village to house railway staff and their families.

Following his appointment in August 1837, Daniel Gooch had been busy setting up locomotive sheds and repair shops at West Drayton and Paddington as well as doing his best to assemble a fleet of workable engines from the ones already ordered by Brunel. With the opening of the railway fast approaching, Gooch also turned his attention to the urgent need to have a central workshop to maintain the locomotive fleet.

It is thought Brunel and Gooch had visited Swindon in 1840, identifying land situated in a triangle between the GWR main line and the new Cheltenham line. Although Reading or Didcot had also been considered, on 13 September Gooch wrote to Brunel recommending Swindon as the location for a 'principal engine establishment'. He argued it was an ideal site as engines were changed there for the steeply graded section westwards towards Chippenham and Box and it was already a junction for the Cheltenham line. He also noted that coal and coke could be delivered to the works by the nearby Wilts & Berks Canal 'at a reasonable price', and that the canal could also be a useful source of water if required.

In February 1841, reporting that operating agreements with the Bristol & Exeter and Cheltenham & GW Union railways would necessarily mean more rolling stock and maintenance work, directors authorised construction of the engine establishment and repair shops, a station and refreshment rooms at Swindon, as well as 'cottages etc. for the residence of many persons employed in the service of the company'. With work on the railway already over budget, the directors noted that the company would only pay for the construction of

New Swindon in 1849. This watercolour panorama, now displayed at the STEAM Museum, was produced by Edward Snell, who began work at Swindon as a fitter in 1843, rising to be assistant works manager in 1846.

The interior of Swindon's first engine house. Capable of housing up to forty-eight engines, this magnificent building used a traverser to access each locomotive bay. The building was swept away in the latter part of the nineteenth century.

workshops, while the station, refreshment rooms and houses for the workforce would be built at the expense of contractors J & D Rigby. Although the arrangement seemed financially expedient at the time, it was one that would have a rather less successful outcome for the GWR in due course.

With the opening of the railway imminent, Brunel and Gooch were faced with the task of designing, building and equipping not only a large engineering workshop complex that would be used for both maintenance and heavy repairs of locomotives, but also a large shed for the engines running trains on the main line and Cheltenham branch. A temporary building was in use by the end of December 1841, and when fully completed in 1846 the new shed could house at least forty-eight locomotives and tenders. The works took another year to complete; while heavy machinery supplied by the Whitworth Company of Manchester was in operation at the end of November 1842, the works was not properly opened until 2 January 1843.

By the early 1850s the engineering heart of Brunel's broad gauge system had grown steadily. At the core of Swindon Works was a series of buildings grouped around three sides of a courtyard, handling the maintenance and repair of locomotives, completed in 1843. The works had a staff complement of over 400 that reflected its dual role of engine shed and workshops; as a result there were ninety-eight footplate staff and sixty-five cleaners, as well as fitters, turners and erectors, coppersmiths, blacksmiths and boilermakers. Staff worked a 57½-hour week, starting at 6am and finishing at 6pm, except on Saturday, when work ceased at 1pm.

Despite financial difficulties suffered by the GWR in the aftermath of its opening, Swindon continued to grow as the new network expanded and traffic increased. New buildings housing blacksmiths, machine and turning shops were subsequently added, along with another courtyard north of the main complex for new smithies and steam hammers.

The west yard of the works, including the building now occupied by the STEAM Museum, seen in 1860.

This stone carving of a GWR 'Firefly' class locomotive was originally fixed to the wall of Brunel's engine house, but is now situated on the building that was the main works offices, currently home to English Heritage.

A plan of Swindon Works in 1846, showing its layout following the initial development stage.

Finally, another range of workshops was added to the west side of the works, accommodating facilities for wagon repair and construction.

The start of wagon building in October 1843 provided the first clue that Swindon was to be more than a maintenance and repair facility; the construction of new locomotives

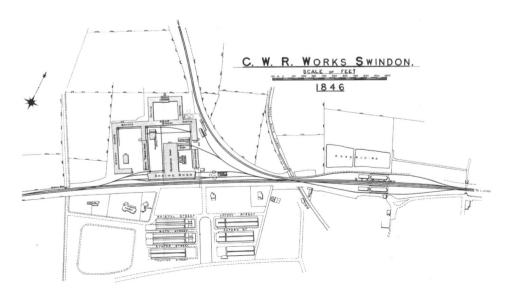

C. W. R. WORKS SWINDON.
SCALE OF FEET
1846

would follow, but not before the GWR had invested in the technology necessary to do this, including a Nasmyth steam hammer, lifting apparatus and other equipment. Evidence of this new direction was the completion of 'Premier', the first of a series of twelve 0-6-0 goods engines in February 1846. The boiler had been purchased from Robert Stephenson so the engine was not the first to be entirely built at the works, but within months the first complete Swindon-built engine had been produced.

In response to the 'Battle of the Gauges' and the establishment of the Gauge Commission in 1845, Gooch was instructed to build a 'colossal locomotive working with all speed'. Within thirteen weeks, Gooch and his staff had produced the 'Great Western', a powerful 2-2-2 that first ran on 1 April 1846. The following year, the first Gooch 8-foot single 'Iron Duke' was built, and while the railway still employed external contractors to manufacture locomotives for some time, Swindon became the main centre for broad gauge engine manufacture. Gooch resigned in 1864 to become GWR chairman, and his successor as locomotive

An engraving showing locomotive boilers being manufactured at Swindon in 1852. The image was reproduced in the *Illustrated Exhibitor*, describing Swindon as a railway works of 'magnitude and extent'.

One of the surviving broad gauge era buildings at Swindon Works, seen in 2017. Built using limestone from the Box area, this building was originally occupied by blacksmiths, and is now offices.

superintendent was Joseph Armstrong. By the time he was appointed, the number of broad gauge locomotives had peaked at around 400; but times were changing, and with the acquisition of standard gauge companies like the West Midland and increasing mixed gauge operation, the number of standard engines running on these lines was growing.

By the early 1870s, with the wholesale conversion of the broad gauge imminent, a huge programme of new standard gauge construction began, and broad gauge building diminished. In the thirteen years of his reign, Armstrong oversaw the building of around 600 standard gauge engines, with a further 250 being built at Wolverhampton; in the same period, sixty-three broad gauge engines were scrapped, leaving only 297 in operation.

Until the 1860s the Great Western had no centralised location for the construction or repair of its carriages; broad gauge carriages had largely been built by contractors and maintained at Paddington, while standard gauge stock was built at Saltney and Worcester. When proposals made to establish a carriage works at Oxford fell through in 1865, land at Swindon was made available to accommodate a carriage works and operations were consolidated there. By the end of 1869 the works was in full operation, and new Swindon-built carriages entered traffic in June that year.

Swindon Works was to play one final role in the broad gauge story. Armstrong died 'in harness' in 1877. The first task of his replacement, William Dean, was to continue the innovation introduced by Armstrong the previous year, of building 'convertible' standard gauge locomotives fitted with lengthened axles to enable them to run on broad gauge lines until their demise.

Just over ten years later a larger, more difficult undertaking for Swindon was planning for the extinction of the broad gauge; while the gradual conversion of lines across the network had taken place for some time, when the date of the final abolition was confirmed as May 1892, Swindon was prepared to house broad gauge locomotives, carriages and wagons displaced by the final conversion. Additional land had to be purchased, and when it was estimated that around 16 miles of sidings would be needed, scrap rail

A GWR official postcard view of 'Bulkeley', one of the last broad gauge engines to be built at the workshops in July 1880.

and sleepers were collected from around the system to accommodate rolling stock.

Nearly 200 engines, over 550 carriages and more than 3,000 wagons ended up at the works, and following the weekend of 21/22 May 1892 the workforce set about converting or scrapping broad gauge stock. There was much to do, but by the end of the year work was well advanced and only ninety-three engines, fifty-seven carriages and 509 wagons remained; by the middle of 1893 work was complete, and with the exception of two locomotives, 'North Star' and 'Lord of the Isles', the broad gauge was no more.

One of the last passenger tank engines built for the broad gauge. '3548' was built at Swindon in November 1888 and converted to standard gauge in November 1892.

Staff at Swindon station had watched the last broad gauge trains pass on that fateful weekend. It had become a busy location by then, but was still suffering the implications of the original decision to allow contractor J & C Rigby to build the station and refreshment rooms at their own expense. An important caveat to the ninety-nine-year legal agreement was that, in return, Rigby's would retain profits from the refreshment rooms and hotel they built. In addition, the GWR

had rashly agreed that all trains to and from London would be compelled to stop at Swindon for ten minutes, allowing passengers to take refreshment.

Despite the handsome accommodation provided by Rigby's, the refreshment rooms at Swindon soon became notorious for all the wrong reasons. The contract was sublet to Samuel Griffiths of Cheltenham, who presided over an operation famous for poor quality food and service. Griffiths resisted attempts to give up the lease, and it was sold outright in 1848. Matters improved under new management, but it was the ten-minute stop that provided the company with the greatest concern. As services became faster, having to halt all express services between London and Bristol proved more than an annoyance. Attempts to ignore the ruling were met with legal action, and it was not until 1895 that the company ended the pain by buying out the lease for £100,000, an expensive finale to a story dating back to the very beginning of Brunel's broad gauge.

The last broad gauge service reaches Swindon station on 20 May 1892. A crowd had also gathered there in 1895, when the first non-stop passenger train passed through.

LOCOMOTIVES AND ROLLING STOCK

LESS THAN A year after the Great Western Railway bill had been approved by Parliament, and several months before the announcement by directors that the new railway would be built to his broad gauge rather than Stephenson's 4-foot 8½-inch gauge, Brunel had written to almost all reputable locomotive builders in the country. He gave them a generalised letter of specification, asking them to provide the GWR with designs for engines to work his new line.

Brunel's letters of June 1836 argued that manufacturers should have the chance to provide designs without detailed specifications from the company, adding that 'the particular form and construction of your engines will be left to your judgement'. Materials and workmanship were to be 'of the very best description', and similar to the 'best engines' used on the Liverpool & Manchester Railway. There were, however, specific requirements laid down by the engineer that caused locomotive builders difficulties and ultimately led to a rather strange selection of engines being delivered to the new railway. Engines should be able to run at 30mph with a relatively slow piston speed of 280 feet per minute, with six-wheeled locomotives to weigh only 10½ tons; boiler pressure was also set at 50 pounds per square inch.

Manufacturers could only comply with these parameters by building engines with small boilers and cylinders and large driving wheels, with the result that most were short of steam and power, and at best capable of only just being

OPPOSITE
A young Daniel Gooch, first locomotive superintendent of the Great Western Railway, portrayed next to a model of his 'Firefly' class locomotive. The model is now in the collection of the National Railway Museum.

able to propel themselves along, let alone pull a train. These unorthodox 'freaks' built as a result of Brunel's insistence on controlling every aspect of the design of his new railway showed his expertise was perhaps not as comprehensive as he had thought. Although nineteen locomotives were produced to Brunel's specification, many proved so unsatisfactory that they were withdrawn very quickly. Of the six engines built by Mather Dixon, for example, 'Mercury' survived the longest, in service for just over four years; the ill-fated 'Mars' lasted only eight months.

None of the engines built to Brunel's specifications had been delivered when the GWR board appointed Daniel Gooch as the company's locomotive superintendent in August 1837. The twenty-one-year-old Gooch was the antithesis of Brunel; having worked in Scotland, South Wales, Lancashire and at Stephenson's works at Newcastle, he already had plenty of practical experience with steam locomotives. As the weird and wonderful selection of engines began to arrive, Gooch spent long hours struggling to keep them running.

The only exceptions were two engines supplied by the Stephenson Company that had not been built to Brunel's

'Vulcan', built by the Tayleur Company and delivered to the GWR on 30 November 1837, hauled the first scheduled passenger train on the GWR on 4 June 1838 'not very successfully'. It was heavily rebuilt and is seen here with 6-foot driving wheels, not the original 8-foot wheels.

specifications anyway, having been intended for the 5-foot 6-inch-gauge New Orleans & Carrollton Railroad in the United States. When the order was cancelled, Brunel was able to acquire them, and the 'North Star' and 'Morning Star' were converted to 7-foot gauge. Both were of a 2-2-2 wheel arrangement and examples of Stephenson's successful 'Patentee' design.

At over 18 tons, both engines were heavier than most built to Brunel's original specification but, as a consequence, had considerably more power and adhesion. Six months after being delivered by canal to Maidenhead in 1837, 'North Star' hauled the first GWR passenger service, a Directors' Special, on 31 May 1838. The reliability and power of the engines resulted in further 'Stars' being ordered from Stephenson, but Gooch's own 'Firefly' design, built between 1840 and 1842, was based on Stephenson practice, with the same 'sandwich' outside frames and 7-foot driving wheels. With the GWR yet to build its own engines, another sixty-two of these locomotives were built by seven different manufacturers; three companies also built twenty-one of the similar but smaller 'Sun' class engines in the same period.

The replica 'Firefly' locomotive seen at its public launch on 3 April 2005 at Didcot Railway Centre. The project to build the engine had taken more than twenty years to complete.

Following the construction of twenty-two 'Leo' and 'Hercules' class engines in 1842, no new locomotives were built for four years, with the 'Firefly' class handling most of the trains in the early years. After the completion of the GWR, the railway was short of money to invest in new engines, and following the 'Gauge War' and the 1845 Royal Commission, it might have been expected that broad gauge locomotive development would wane. Following the stay of execution given by the Commission in allowing the GWR to continue with the broad gauge, Gooch was asked to produce more

The original 'Iron Duke' locomotive was completed in April 1847. This replica was produced by the Science Museum to celebrate the 150th anniversary of the GWR in 1985.

powerful engines. The 2-2-2 'Great Western' was essentially an enlarged 'Firefly', and the first locomotive to be built at the company's new workshops at Swindon.

Within months, the more powerful 4-2-2 'Iron Duke' class appeared. These engines would haul expresses on the GWR main line until the 1870s, when they were extensively renewed. The growth of the broad gauge network in Wales, the West of England and elsewhere meant that more motive power was required. Between 1846 and 1864, 235 Gooch designs were built, most at Swindon, and to handle increased freight business on the railway no fewer than 102 of these were 0-6-0 goods engines. From his earliest days as locomotive superintendent, Gooch had used standardised fittings and components for his engines, quickly seeing that it would reduce costs and make maintenance easier.

Gooch's successor Joseph Armstrong was only responsible for three broad gauge designs. By the time he took control in 1864 the Northern Division of the GWR had become

'Mammoth' was one of six goods engines designed by Gooch that formed part of the 'Pyracmon' class and was built at Swindon in April 1848. A 1930s GWR publication noted that this drawing came from Gooch's sketchbook.

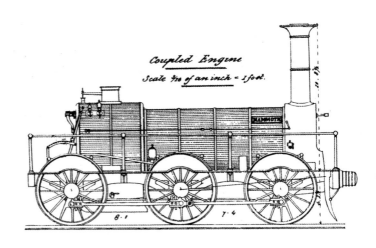

One of Pearson's eight 4-2-4 well tank locomotives built for the Bristol & Exeter Railway. These amazing-looking locomotives had 8-foot 10-inch diameter driving wheels and large bell-mouthed chimneys.

predominantly standard gauge in character, whilst the broad gauge was concentrated on Swindon, the old Bristol to London main line and the West Country. Armstrong locomotives comprised twenty-six 'Hawthorn' class 2-4-0 tender engines, fourteen 'Swindon' class 0-6-0 goods engines and the more unusual tank engines of the 'Sir Watkin' class built to run on the Metropolitan and Hammersmith & City lines in London. These were the last new broad gauge engines to be constructed at Swindon, apart from the reconstruction of 'Iron Duke' 4-2-2s from 1871 to 1888. Although officially classed as 'Renewals' by the GWR, it is thought that only the first three engines of what became known as the 'Rover' class contained any original parts, the remaining twenty-one being completely new.

The completion of the final three 'Rover' locomotives was supervised by William Dean, who had replaced Armstrong in 1877; although the end of the broad gauge was in sight, services were still running and engines were still needed. As a result 111 locomotives built before 1892 were 'convertibles' which could be rebuilt to run on the 4-foot 8½-inch-gauge at a later date.

Towards the end of the Armstrong era, many of the independent companies that had been part of Brunel's broad gauge network were finally absorbed into the GWR. Although a number had over the years been directly operated by the Great Western, the Bristol & Exeter, Cornwall, South Devon, Torbay & Brixham and Vale of Neath railways all had locomotive fleets of their own and almost 200 engines were finally taken into GWR ownership by 1876.

There is not space here to do more than mention some of the more significant and unusual engines operated by these railways. The Bristol & Exeter Railway, which had been operated by the GWR until 1849, had a large complement of 119 engines, and its own locomotive workshops at Bristol. The most famous engines were undoubtedly the 4-2-4 express tank locomotives designed by the railway's locomotive superintendent James Pearson. With 8-foot 10-inch driving wheels and a top speed of 80mph they had a relatively short life, four being rebuilt with tenders after 1876.

The failure of Brunel's atmospheric system on the South Devon in 1848 had led to a period of operation by the GWR, but the company subsequently acquired its own complement of more than eighty locomotives. From 1859 the SDR also entered into agreements to work both the Cornwall and West Cornwall railways, maintaining its fleet from workshops at Newton Abbot. The steep gradients and tight curves of West Country lines meant that passenger and goods locomotives were tank engines, many built by the Bristol company Avonside.

Two final companies absorbed had engines that were taken into the locomotive fleet; the Vale of Neath Railway contributed just nineteen engines when the railway became part of the Great Western in 1866. All were saddle tank designs, the first a 4-4-0 built in 1851 by the Stephenson Company, and the last a 0-6-0 built by Slaughter &

'Tiny' pictured on the platform at Newton Abbot Station in May 1975. The 1868 locomotive is the only surviving broad gauge locomotive, thought to have been used for shunting in the yard at Newton Abbot until the 1880s.

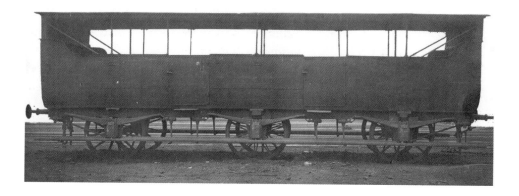

Gruning in Bristol a decade later. The Torbay & Brixham Railway only had two 0-4-0 tank engines when it was taken over by the GWR in January 1883, more than enough to work the 2-mile-long branch.

GWR iron bodied Third Class carriage built around 1844.

In the early days of the GWR, broad gauge rolling stock was purchased from outside contractors; a number of four-wheeled carriages were supplied to the railway but soon proved unsuitable, and six-wheeled vehicles became the standard until bogie coaches were built in the 1860s. The accommodation provided for travellers depended on class; first-class carriages tended to have four compartments, described by one writer as 'snug little boxes'. Carriage windows were glazed, unlike those in second class; the same writer noted that those travelling in 'well ventilated' second-class carriages would 'amuse themselves on the journey by extracting cinders from each other's eyes'. In both first and second class the wheels were encased in iron splashers inside the carriage, providing a trip hazard for the unwary passenger peering through the gloom of the unlit interior.

An early *Bradshaw's Guide* announced that third-class passengers on the GWR would 'be conveyed by the goods trains', and while other railways treated this class of traveller similarly, the accommodation provided was sparse at best. As a result of Gladstone's 1844 'Cheap Trains Act' the open trucks used before this date were replaced with six-wheeled carriages that were hardly more than goods wagons fitted with a roof; each had ten transverse bench seats with no backs and only one door on each side, meaning passengers had to climb over the seats to find a place.

Later carriages were more sophisticated and comfortable, and the sensation of travelling in a broad gauge express was described as 'majestic but lumbering'. As the conversion of Brunel's 7-foot gauge approached, Swindon turned out increasing numbers of convertible carriages that were in essence standard gauge coach bodies with broad gauge underframes that could be replaced when the conversion was completed.

Some indication of Brunel's insular view of his broad gauge system was the fact that goods wagons provided for the earliest trains did not have any identification. He argued it was 'improbable' that 'they would ever leave the Great Western system'. Initially only two types of wagon were provided. Open 'box' wagons were flat wagons into which containers carrying goods could be loaded. 'Tilt' wagons had semi-circular ends with hops over which tarpaulins could be stretched. Initially, trains consisted of only these two types of wagon, but as traffic began to grow, further variations were built. By 1854 there were more than 3,000 broad gauge wagons, a figure that had grown to over 5,600 almost ten years later. By then the figure included more than 1,000 open wagons and cattle trucks, 2,023 covered vans and 2,100 coal, coke and other miscellaneous wagons.

BELOW LEFT
This replica second-class carriage shows that while passengers were at least protected from the elements by a roof, there was no glass in the windows to keep out the wind and rain.

BELOW RIGHT
Remains of a broad gauge carriage slowly rotting away in a Gloucestershire garden, photographed in 1967.

FURTHER READING

Awdry, Christopher. *Brunel's Broad Gauge Railway*. OPC, 1992.

Brindle, Steven. *Brunel: The Man Who Built the World*. Weidenfeld & Nicholson, 2005.

Bryan, Tim. *Brunel: The Great Engineer*. Ian Allan, 1999.

Cattell, John & Falconer, Keith. *Swindon: The Legacy of a Railway Town*. HMSO, 1995.

Chapman, W.G. *Track Topics*. GWR, 1935.

Day, Lance. *Broad Gauge*. HMSO, 1985.

Jolly, Mike & Garmsworthy, Paul. *The Broad Gauge in Cornwall*. Broad Gauge Society, 1995.

Peck, Alan. *The Great Western at Swindon Works*. OPC, 1983.

Railway Correspondence & Travel Society. *The Locomotives of the Great Western Railway Part Two: Broad Gauge*. RCTS, 1952.

Sheppard, Geof. *Broad Gauge Locomotives*. Noodle Books, 2008.

Vaughan, Adrian. *A Pictorial Record of Great Western Architecture*. OPC, 1977.

Waters, Laurence. *The Great Western Broad Gauge*. OPC, 1999.

Williams, Archibald. *Brunel & After: The Romance of the Great Western Railway*. GWR, 1925.

The 'Iron Duke' replica locomotive is now resident at the Great Western Society's Didcot Railway Centre awaiting restoration. The engine was seen there in August 2017.

PLACES TO VISIT

The Broad Gauge Society: the society promotes research into the 7-foot ¼-inch railways of Britain in the nineteenth century and holds meetings, field trips and model exhibitions as well as producing a magazine and supporting other historic publications. Details of membership are available at www.broadgauge.org.uk

There are numerous examples of surviving broad gauge era stations and structures, such as Bristol Temple Meads, Paddington and the Royal Albert Bridge as well as smaller structures such as stations at Charlbury and Culham.

The broad gauge story is also told in museums and railway sites:

Didcot Railway Centre, Didcot, Oxfordshire OX11 7NJ. Telephone: 01235 817200.
Website: www.didcotrailwaycentre.org.uk Home to the Great Western Society, Didcot Railway Centre has recreated a section of broad gauge railway, incorporating mixed and broad gauge track and the transhipment shed built at Didcot in the 1850s. Both the 'Firefly' and 'Iron Duke' replica locomotives are also in residence. The society also displays a broad gauge wagon turntable originally from Devonport Dockyard and a section of South Devon Railway atmospheric railway pipe.
STEAM: Museum of the Great Western Railway, Firefly Drive, Swindon SN2 2EY. Telephone: 01793 466646. Website: www.steam-museum.org.uk STEAM is housed in a building dating back to the broad gauge era at Swindon Railway Works. There are many broad gauge items in its collections, most famously the replica 'North Star' built in 1925 to replace the 1837 original. The museum also has broad gauge signals, locomotive

nameplates and much else. Outside the museum are surviving Brunel-era buildings, now occupied by English Heritage and other organisations.

South Devon Railway Trust Museum, The Station, Buckfastleigh, Devon, TQ11 0DZ. Tel: 01364 644370. Website: www.southdevonrailway.co.uk The museum is home to 'Tiny', the only surviving broad gauge engine, built in 1868, for many years displayed on the platform at Newton Abbot Station.

A further drawing of navvies involved in the final conversion of the broad gauge in Cornwall, originally reproduced in the *Graphic* magazine of 28 May 1892.

INDEX